icehockeying

Peter Oberfrank – Hunziker

Impressum:

Bibliografische Information der Deutschen
Nationalbibliothek: Die Deutsche Nationalbibliothek
verzeichnet diese Publikation in der Deutschen
Nationalbibliografie; detaillierte bibliografische Daten sind im
Internet über www.dnb.de abrufbar.

© 2021 Peter Oberfrank - Hunziker

Herstellung und Verlag

BoD - Books on Demand, Norderstedt

ISBN 9783754331231

NHL tampy celebratingly ..... Peter
Oberfrank - Hunziker as happy daddy
heartily celebrating unique indiany sporty
being and remembering great celebrating
and hearty being and working and russian
icehockeyplaying ..... confetti parties and
Puddingfestival disco musical nature
showing and partying and fashion shows
and smiling and laughing and sportying
and icehockeying with all my NHL art
names like NHL spacy indiany 24
Perthaler and 99 Wayne Gretzky and
Vasilvesky and Dallas Stars and New York
Islanders and New York Rangers
celebratingly and 47 Martin St. Louis and
Yanni Gourdet and ÖFB and OEHV and
american indiany and Yagr and Indiany and
NHL 79 Ross Colton ..... NHL Tampa Bay
Ligthning is really ever highligthning with
happy smiling and easy being and heartily
being .... Peter Oberfrank - Hunziker